WORK & PLAY

WORK & PLAY

OWEN BULLOCK

RECENT
WORK
PRESS

Work & Play
Recent Work Press
Canberra, Australia

Copyright © Owen Bullock 2017

ISBN: 9780648087878 (paperback)

A catalogue record for this
book is available from the
National Library of Australia

All rights reserved. This book is copyright. Except for private study, research, criticism or reviews as permitted under the Copyright Act, no part of this book may be reproduced, stored in a retrieval system, or transmitted in any form by any means without prior written permission. Enquiries should be addressed to the publisher.

Cover illustration: 'Behind the Red Ball' by Christopher Woo, reproduced under Creative Commons licence 2.0
Cover design: Recent Work Press
Set in Bembo Std

recentworkpress.com

Contents

Yeah. Yeah, that's it, bro	1
46	2
Thoughts bother the night	3
She belongs nowhere	4
Five hard cover books	5
I'm superman	6
Which way is the narrative heading?	7
the pig the lips the skin	8
Num num	9
fleshier with age	10
I'm tendrils today	11
'Poetry' with an accent	12
Creativity's a wild pig	13
eraserself	14
Let someone else be crazy	15
definitions of play	16
Bubble	17
Spec	18
He made an inventory	19
The pipe eased his mind	20
You visited	21
Proems	22
ania i	23
A mouthful of air	24
when they put me through the mill	25
He had a stroke last April	26
At the bus stop	27
Chest	28
He hid inside a ball	29
The fool's cap	30
Installing	31
Coaching tips	32
New playlist 1 & 2	33

Layers	34
Brogo, Bega	37
Spring	41
repechage	42
Surdity	43
guide	44
suburb, Torbay	45
working space	46
this lark	47
coming of age	50
building blocks	51
towards	54
lost, found, lost ...	55
the fourteenth of May	56
line	57
the candidate	58
displace	60
alarms	61
lips du	63
Ox	64
A dozen limmered ticks	67
work & play	69
a prison for magicians	70
Voodoo Chile (slight return)	71

Yeah. Yeah, that's it, bro. He had a skinful. Yeah. I couldn't tell, just had this feeling, you know? Back of me head. No, I never been there before. But I knew that's where the horse would go.

People say, I've looked a hundred times—usually in the same places. So I look where they don't think it could be, and there it is.

46

Forty-six years and never opened eyes underwater. This the sea and there was salt. The day I forced myself. A morning swim, before the heat. Time with you. Sand at our feet stretched, connected to beaches in Cornwall, Wales, places lodged. Colours and mists, fragments, shell. Now at each river and shore I see what I'm swimming in. That day we heard your brother died.

Thoughts bother the night, they're out of control. He tells himself the things he's thinking about, lecture, meeting, poem, have already happened. He stops thinking and sleeps. Next day, on his way to an event he tells himself it's already happened. It messes with his head, the body feels a kind of loss, a lack of excitement, but it's useful.

She belongs nowhere

She moved a lot as a child, father a diplomat. Loves to throw out, get a new flat. Shelves books at the library when she's agitated, though she doesn't work there anymore. Reads fast, the details of a life. Her flatmate beside, watching her intuit. They celebrate with Christmas pudding and custard. That's breakfast.

Five hard cover books

Robinson Crusoe, the copy Gran gave him, with shaggy-haired illustrations, from the old books of Granfer's. That had a smell. Had been to the mine. Precious Bane, which made him cry each time he read, 'I've chosen my bit of Paradise. Tis on your breast, my dear acquaintance.' The Selected Poems of Emily Dickinson, discrete and blue, magic and personified. To which he wrote a letter in reply. The needling collection of Chinese poetry; pages seemed to pierce his skin, but the binding was defence. The eagerly awaited Harry Potter and the Order of the Phoenix, which despite one slightly long-winded explanation by Dumbledore, was not too long.

I'm superman. I fly through space, beat up the bad guys and make them surrender. But I can't seem to solve the arms problem or stop so many individuals owning guns, I guess because at bottom human nature likes to hurt others. I guess ultimately the answer is education, so I should get a B Ed. or something equivalent.

Which way is the narrative heading?

The narrative is walking through Europe towards Greece. It recently acquired a donkey, which gives the protagonist something to talk to. It began on the Comino, the sociable solitary and the feet, one, one and one, the sense of wandering. Heading east, the protagonist returns to New Zealand and Australia, but not before meeting a monk who wears Levis and tends the hooves of animals with an omniscient first person; a Welsh dance teacher who makes origami, speaking to the listener with their own speech mannerisms; an Indian cook who dices vegetables with the honesty of a teenager. The narrative is almost home now.

the pig the lips the skin the eventual gravestone with you rubbing on it I shouldn't say but keep colouring what goes into the sky a flamingo I haven't seen but watched pelicans trawl and flesh, fetch and eat I don't know if I could put that black shirt on him

Num num, birdy num-nums, nom du nom. Creosote, croeso, welcome, willkommen, Belconnen (Belco-nin). Nom du nom. Nom nom. Numb numb. Umyum. The Republic of Umyum—his fantasy. The pixie forest, pixie-dundle on duty, watching the road for strangers who seldom come. Dreams of Jodhpur and Miscreant in search of the Sacred Barrel. He shall never realise. Num.

fleshier with age, the word like a weapon. flashes and points, deflects and rebounds, back into the quiver. our safety, defence. time thrusts by air. we record its passing with arms, with legs, with torso. a recall soon as echo, soon as past. a bite when we don't take the fruit. a taste, a flip of the tongue. a warning ssshhhuhh leaves us with an undertaking understanding of the body left here.

I'm tendrils today. Speak to me, I'll write a poem. Show me the bark, I'll plant you a tree. Crash me skyblue, I'll comfort you a cloud. Stand at the bus reading a novel, I'll oratorio right back at you in a strange and distant land she stood like no other fearless in the face of contumely. Take me to song and record a melody, I'll be grounded.

'Poetry' with an accent

It would help if poetry didn't accost me before i got to my desk with a delicate found line if it didn't ambush me as i ventured to the fridge with an inspiring conversation if it didn't crash my email before i had a chance to rave about what inspired me if poetry didn't condense its energy into the lustre of the polished stone from Paihia if poetry wasn't waiting at the bus stop at the lights on the bus in the shape of the old man with a triple comb-over in the shape of the woman who interrupts our conversation with the statement 'I think sometimes people just need space!'

Creativity's a wild pig that comes at you out of the bush when you're isolated without a gun and uncertain of the knife in your hand. If someone were to control it, it would be a tame event, a habit. We die each day because we live.

eraserself

inspired by L.A. Hindmarsh's self-exposure

I am not a beautiful man sitting in the garden of secrets with a tumbler of flower petals
I am not a castrated faun rediscovering Glam Rock with philanthropist overtones
I am not a swimsuit doubling for a parachute
I am not an emblazoned eagle ready to die for the burger stand that offers the best 2-for-1
I am not asking for more by wanting to give, wanting to create

Let someone else be crazy

I was starting to get jittery, back and forth to the printing room with slight but important revisions, to the balcony to read, the desk to correct, when a man came in, sat at a cubicle, talked aloud to himself, ran frantic to the printer, exclaiming *yes, that's it* and *fuck*, and I got on with what I should have been doing, let someone else be the crazy one today.

definitions of play

doing something that isn't there; making it up, seeing what happens, for the sake of; inviting, inviting others to join, playing games, making rules, revising breaking rules, assembling, destroying; going inside, finding out who isn't there, finding out a god isn't there, finding out; creating perceiving the world, translating self to outside and outside to self; following colours, sounds, the feeling of heartbeat, following sand on skin, milk on body, mud on face, piss on legs; telling lies, telling *telling* lies; not caring, climbing trees, jumping ditches, frightening the dog, tempting the snake, tempting fate, burning bridges; failing, it makes you.

Bubble

Why don't you talk about the river you skimmed on, the child's lips disappearing in the distance, imminent rock, water you merged with, balancing, what sound was called between you, how you fought the rapids, how the stuttering made you birth inside another, float together, anchored twice, spilling each, bubbles.

Spec

for Rebecca Devon-Sillett

As you come to the end of the chapter I'll shriek the zagareet. When the characters take off in a direction you didn't expect I'll sound the vuvuzela. When you mine some pithy dialogue I'll give a taut *ooohh*. When the lovers come together I'll utter a strangled *yes*. Leap to my feet. Thrust my arms in the air calling *Starfish*! like Bill Bailey. When the kid solves the problem without adult intervention I'll drift off and fix my own life. Writing's my favourite spectator sport.

He made an inventory of men assassinated by King Edward; gathered stone, beams and thatching to restore the cottage; attended rebels who stormed garrisons, wound and unwound bandages; mended shields, retrieved frightened horses; procured weapons and necessaries, Wallace.

The pipe eased his mind. Thoughts of his beloved cat, endless rows with his wife, the garden, human manure. Not having anyone to share his vision with ... he never had one before ... when it arrived like a rainy morning and wouldn't leave it was too late.

You visited, as no-one else in the family had; played with the children, knitted toys and folded hankies into mice; let them into the caravan with the password 'cup of tea'; welcomed my wife; accepted my deviating path; gave me money for gigs and football matches; introduced me to friends, at their level, boasted of my achievements; took me to relatives; knitted jerseys; washed me when I wet myself, yes, screamed, and gave birth to me.

Proems

for Subhash Jaireth

Proems are hand grenades you say throwing one to me what was firm ground is rubble I twist on broken concrete torn turfs the sign from the street you laugh entering a shop you're about to hold up in case it still has iambs even they can come in handy you leave your bag of punctuation at the op shop drop the little rulers you used to draw line endings into a busker's hat they collapse into coins small change the intention's what matters

ania i

she held me she cried to me entreated me i screamed me when she finished me the energy robert bly told me i can die happy i heard ania walwicz my daughter passed mechanics my son singing songs my daughter painting portraits finished gypsy wagon eeeeeeeeeee

i clear the drive i mulch trees i stake i oil the shed i swim in stream i snorkel i see cockabullies i find crayfish i feel the eel i saw up old pine i chop wood i clean the tent i pack away i go back to the city i wake at four i meditate i write i mess up i study

A mouthful of air

for Malachi Doyle

Where we end. Or begin. A fragment. Mouthful of air. Food. Chatter. Refectory. Concern expressed by a voice; rejection of a gesture. Gamble. Gulp the slapping shore of Lake Burley-Griffin, cheer flocks in grand formation at Bermagui; couples for life. Pure water on a Bega hillside. Perhaps you pass before you find it, but it takes you high: one last rarefied mouthful.

when they put me through the mill, words came out, some meditative, some loving, some detailed. they threw the meditative words on the scrap pile, chewed the words of love like tobacco and spat them out after lunch. kept the details.

He had a stroke last April, another one this month, but no seizures for a while. His mate's there, making tea, fetching sandwiches. Nurses, managers, ambulance crew, cleaners, anaesthetists, surgeons ... circulate. Monkey could do my job, the orderly says. Couldn't manage without you, mate. Well you take care, mate. Thanks, all the best.

At last, here comes a doctor.

At the bus stop

He's to go to the dentist, shows me his teeth. He went up to Oberon for the steam rally. His uncle's building a shed and they're trying to stop it. Canberra's not a bad place when you get used to it. He's been here all his life, 43 in a couple of months, sixteen years in the supermarket. I've seen you there, I say. Yeah, they can never get enough staff. He flinches at blaring vehicles, asks me if I drive. He hasn't for eight years. One of his psychiatrists told him he should never have got a licence, can't concentrate. He could do it if he had to.

Chest

Jake said he'd give tea-chest bass a go. That year he played drums in an experimental rock band was the happiest of his life—a pro drummer who'd drummed for Chuck Berry said he was the best 'non-drummer' he'd ever heard. None of the stress of remembering lyrics. But the heavy, single string blistered his index finger. He took to wearing a gardening glove and liked the sense of protection, of hugging, the kind that clung. A rubber glove gave an interesting, strangled tone for sliding notes. A surgical glove got an even better twang but broke easily. He kept a shoe box of options. Soon it was a sack. He needed to be able to get at them more easily at gigs. He built a rack that looked like so many wind chimes, but they were gloves. He started wearing makeup, KISS meets Cleopatra. Audiences cheered the fashionista director of entertainment, waited in fascination as he re-clad his hands. The fatal moment, he sliced a finger open with a band saw making another frame. No amount of bandaging or layering of gloves would assuage.

He hid inside a ball, the juggler found it. Mill's Mess made him dizzy; the Shower lashed boredom. He made a new game: keeping arms and feet splayed wide, sprung off the wall rap rap rapidly. He was starshaped. Hands and feet wore down, limbs shivered and cracked, spun about, shaved to stunted. Shrunk to a ball. Fit. In.

The fool's cap was full of sheets of paper. When I reached my hand in, something bit me, skin torn from bone. The fool laughed, offered a salve. The hand healed quickly. I followed him, took money as he performed on the streets, watched as he milked the wealthy for attention, courted favour for position in the senate. I offered a man my own hat full of sheets of paper. When it bit him he slapped me.

Installing

Jón Páll Sigmarsson's first installation is a mobile phone standing twelve feet high. You type the letter A by pulling down a lever which takes all your strength. Activate letter B by lifting a 30 litre bucket of water from a shelf at chest height. Clock letter C by sawing through a 40cm log with a bow saw. A message can take an hour. The exhibit relays what you've written to a real cellphone which sends the message, though there might be network problems. Sigmarsson's work will be tremendously popular, the gallery owners tell me.

Coaching tips

The first thing we did with the new coach was learn how to juggle. Fucking stupid. But keeping three balls in the air gives you a lot of confidence when you drop back to one. We all had to kick with both feet. The forwards as well as the backs did half-back drills. He made us agree there was no point carrying flab; we got rid of it. We gave up beer. Stopped talking about luck. Finally, we beat the All Blacks.

New playlist 1 & 2

Breathy voice. Lyrics already heard; beat so simple; chords the same. Ephemeral treble-bound synth barely discernible reminds me I'm going to die soon—at least that's something. Welcome to Cloudkid remix.

Swingin, singin, rhythmin. She violins in the garden with her angel wings on. They're shakin the matchbox. *What did you do to me?* Alive. With the Boswell Sisters. *When I take my sugar to tea* sounds like *do tea*.

Layers

We peel the town together; I take walls, you, rooves. In one house a woman hasn't spoken to her partner for four days because he shaved his beard. He didn't understand the emotional security for her in his appearance (at a difficult time); the decision required by the casting director, a true come dream to act in a film. In another room a woman sleeps on the floor because her partner hits her while he's asleep (though never when conscious). We tire of our abilities and walk parks in the early hours. You say, 'I don't know if I want to do this anymore, they all seem so sad, and like mirrors and you worry about yourself ...'

Brogo, Bega

> *for Barbara Curnow*

We're going to Bega.

Broga Bega Broga Bega Broga Broga Broga Bega.

We're staying at Barbara's house.

> sunset—
> swathes of orange lichen
> discarded by angels

Slow. Beside the drive, a wallaby with a bushy tail.

> the crackle
> of walu—
> we've arrived

A dwelling, full of silence. Socked feet find the meditation room.

> in the house
> of characterful doors
> a framed photo
> of a characterful door
>
> the profile
> of the Rayburn's flu
> reminds me ...

Father's pot of tea steeping on the shelf above the hob.

A framed jigsaw ornaments the bathroom; orange & yellow tiles, black & white parrots.

A fireplace worthy of a great hall, well-prepared, flares swiftly.

> perusing someone else's books
> the cuckoos
> in us

"My life is a creative act" – Ram Dass.

Staying in someone else's house is like looking at a portrait for a long time.

> the candle's shadow
> flat
> against the wall
>
> view of the bush
> no more
> overlit corridors
>
> straight eucalypts
> warm warble
> of kookaburra

I want to touch the quiet. Sometimes it seems as though everyone's had a more troubled life than me; nothing attacks me from the past. A bird hovers among ruminations. It's our nature, too, to look for food, to go where the work is—what we've been discussing in our couple of days away from routine.

"Suffering lets us see where our attachments are—and that helps us get free."

We're noticing the physical frustrations of growing older.

"Aging represents failure in our society, so each of us looks ahead and sees inevitable failure."

Driving out on a corrugated road. Wind-shorn flowers, coastal rosemary, sand forms based in erosion. From the headland at Bermagui, peering through the wind.

We freeze on the darkened road home, a wombat waddles across it, and stops. We soak him up.

Trees down the valley sway slightly.

> the peace
> of the mountains
> talking is profane
>
> morning breeze
> only red parrots
> chatter
>
> losing at scrabble
> wanting to get rid of
> some 'I's

Spring

overtaking forks don't indicate

    awwh 'L'!

ride your palanquin

store capacitance

a long, mysterious question

quote chop
something up works

a tick to the beehive
serves animals

    extend customer experiences beyond the browser

mullock
semi-hobo
tender bone

    she's been shoulder-tapped

jaup the propitious light

    it's a good day for rainbows

repechage

a dream is a blue estuary
with a long corridor

people come and go
hidden in mist

a ten-year-old's ambition
erodes the forest where his old self wanders
moors, burras, the burren ...

the glow of houses, streetlights
are more than clusters of gas

lines peer out
flickering, flashing
at the cow's coffin-shaped head

two or three start walking that way
then they all follow

the gate-opener
lingers at the back

Surdity

I ride an igloo to work
a bell chimes, and the Zen priest
holds a typewriter for the monkey
to type his request
to join a reality TV show

where Susan Boyle takes on Wayne Rooney at darts
and Ollie Murrs keeps score
with help from Roger Federer
who's distracted by an old man's dentures
that have fallen from a bar stool

the monkey's job is to get the teeth back in
before the old man starts a singalong
out of time, on shaky feet

Wayne pins his boot to the floor
with a great dart, Susan hums the kazoo solo
Roger applauds the efforts of all
and Ollie pinches the igloo parked outside

for once, the Zen priest doesn't get the joke
and rues the demise of the last company on earth
to make type-writer ribbons

the monkey never leaves the tribal council

guide

> *"watch the waning"* Annora Gollop

stalks wither, cicadas cast shells
bees peter out across floors
the sail-cloth rots; he takes
running and offset measurements
to design a new garden
people walk hand in hand with buildings
say things like *I want to play the pokies*
after experience comes knowing and a theory
but remember the waning
we don't like our lips to shrink
age is knocking
like a priest with no beliefs
a salesman with nothing to sell
a neighbour with an empty plate
and we must still laugh, as the sun laughs

suburb, Torbay

in the space
between others
lemon trees
pongas, fantails
hibiscus, succulents

wash racks
peg bag
hand made
by Grannie

the deck drying

someone plucks a ukulele

a hedge-trimmer roars

a neighbour's bowl sings
as it hits the floor

working space

a wood-louse mimics the faded blue grey of the curtain
I think it's dead

a cough, alive and well

a punchinella mask on the Mexican hat

I question motives
I'm a judge

a cushion on the floor is enough tonight
stuck in tick-tock
bits of food dropped

albedo means light reflected

poems determined by the size of paper

the lamp fitting doesn't work
the spring on your drawing board is stiff
its arm like a giant ratchet

this lark

> *"And the thing itself, not the thing itself."*
> Jean Valentine

> *"What we had, we have."*
> The Duke of Devon, quoted by Jean Valentine

we had marbles
football magazines
posters of Bruce Lee

tapes recorded from the radio
incense
a Pink Floyd bootleg
clear as the studio

out of my body
on meditation
I looked down in panic
never left again

*

awake, solitariness
tolerates
the ramblings of the mind

I hear stories all day
listen, nod & make noises
make noises, listen & nod

no agreeing to be done
I come to premature conclusions
and no one objects

I wander through rooms
like a trespasser
steal bananas
nothing to lose

*

> *"the light that shrivels a mountain
> And leaves a man alive."* Adrienne Rich

the poems I read
make me feel awake
and dreaming

they're indulgent mothers

I allow myself to say
what I miss

*

an email from the day world
comes into the night:
*Did you learn how to open your chakras
in school or college?*

check publications
read the generous report,
the uncertainties
of someone else's journal,
a funny story
on the mentor's blog

make a submission at 3 a.m.
the editor in North America won't say
you're up at strange hours

*

check Daily Affirmations
The more I take care of myself
the more prosperous I am

check bank account
pay's gone in

outside: birdsong
moon, morning star, sunrise

horses galloping
lengths in the paddock

coming of age

he holds in his fingers
the palm of humanity
blotched, wrinkled, hairy
or smooth, milky, thumb-sized

a bee mounts grass stalks
takes off, stumbles
wriggles its abdomen
as if spraying the ground—
it looks like it's dying
already

a brother is lost
and many weep
their grief in proportion
to the love they feel

now
a woman tickles her man
hair shakes in silhouette
it's time to fix the water leak
bury the rat in the shrubbery
boil the kettle
think about the poem

building blocks

1. *red*

sexblood and glory

the nib pits skin

stains cheeks
a blackberry's darkness

chillies the kind of shock
growing up has to be

the carpet's
approval

2. *yellow*

daffodils
smile on the bank above the garden
for mother

she bought
the Leeds United kit

corduroy trousers offended Gran
when they picked her up from Chapel

bright dungarees
weren't wide enough
to hold three babies

the Commer van painted egg-yolk
for a trip around the islands

juggling clubs
spinning the air

van Gogh's
thick palette
confused surfaces

the T-shirt, Queen St
for five dollars
after seven years
beginning to fray

the Queen's wedding suit
with her Bob Dylan hat
and her telegram photo
for Grannie

the angel you gave me
on a string
photographed with my pottery pig
Dorkin Reed
alias Philip Lesser
who writes erotic novels
under a pseudonym
when he goes on holiday
it guides him
somewhere sunny

3. *blue*

efficient, coded
jeaned with boots or sneakers

sea & sky
(death when the sea breaks cover)

to carry on you need a card
stamped and signed
a uniform starched

I own you
'you stay in this family'

blood
bled to the challenge
it detests

4. white

jellyfish
embodied mother
afterlife
at the movies

squirted into a jug
                    frothing

            curdled
      strained for cheese

sauce, saucers
Gran's pinnies
embroidered
not so the walls
      washed
by a reluctant father

surrendered for Indian games
cowboy guns with bone
handles
        a porcelain bath

sighted later
                in awe
opposites
        absorbed

towards

with our jokes about dust, hebes
tai chi classes

the helix of time past
time future
spins, stops in us

we're sewn into memories
like children of older days
into underclothes for winter

memories keep us
but they merge and fade

and we will grey
into the white light
at the end

which they speak about
who died

lost, found, lost …

you told the headmaster
you didn't want to wear green
he said you had to
to go to his school

in the first week
you forged mother's signature
so they only ever saw yours

we shot at rabbits
from the bedroom window
but never hit any

buried money
for a money tree

ate raw sausages
from the fridge, on holiday
in a caravan, a few feet
from mother and father's bed

you grabbed the boy
who bullied me
slammed him against the wall
pick on someone your own size

when I left home at sixteen
you came to visit me
every fortnight

smiled at my baby
didn't scare him

you were the protagonist
in my stories—always a quest
to find you again

the fourteenth of May

the day is grey and cold
for your funeral

I can't concentrate
on anything

watch a leaf
shaken by wind

summer toys
not put away

tick beans coming up in the path
rosemary still flowering

I remove notes and poems
study the estuary

empty of water
peppered with birds

we two will not walk there
my brother

but thoughts of you
lead me

and you speak quietly again
as in my dream

you're doing alright

line

assembled the shed and there was
one piece over

a gift of rain
for the broken hearted

lions roaring
in the suburbs

three calls
to the help desk

why does he do it,
is there no other way?

into space
a rocket
careers

the candidate

"A compromise candidate was elected." Mark Young

he goes on holiday
takes a briefcase

likes to buy new
loose-fitting clothes
when he gets there
give his suit to a street-dweller
(and don't forget the shoes)

blank paper (in the case)
he begins the new erotic novel

dines alone
observing how ...

she stands   removes

a packet of cigarettes from her pocket

takes one

sits   and lights   draws
                         extends a hand

       exhales

gazes across the street   but who knows where?

          the hand with the cigarette   outlined

like a conductor   determining

       rests

her hand   folds inwards

she draws the cigarette   again   lets out a sigh

       smoke   disperses

             a few centimetres
                         from his skin

displace

another hour sanding—
will it ever be finished?
desktop

a hand wrapped up
it feels like forever
the web

breaking the rolling pin
mouse
under the door

the net flashes—
ten cents
per cabbage white

two more
windows gone
garage football

365 miles
game abandoned ...
the hard drive home

crawling in
to hedge camp—
what's the password?

alarms

*I'm a smallish medium
and in China I'm extra large*

> *if I were an author
> I'd write a book called ...*

> *bleeding without glasses*

> *hiding in junk mail*

> *I see a dog in italics*

> *that sounds experiential*

> *it took me to a place
> that I wasn't*

> *initiate the force field!*

> *clouds contain sentient bacteria*

the fire alarm is still singing

found myself in this paper bag
& just kept talking

seek me out
in a well-lit corridor

> *ayayah!*
> the bird calls

wears anti-
facial recognition make-up

    Aint Skeered

        we all self-helped each other

      there will be mummy and daddy words

it throws the potter

lips du

The Matrix was a doco

    alright then, I'll come

        I won't reveal your font secrets

            he gave a soft no

                poetry? I'm so glad the University is doing something as useless as that

                    he's dead with black eyes like fish

I have your lips on me

            eye   aye

Vudu

Ox

that week I left the dishes
vomit bags by my bed

No Pride in Genocide
Fuck Australia Day

he robbed a bank with a cactus

garlic,
if there's garlic!

flags in the ant hills

her family
had Sean Connery for their milk boy
shaken not curdled

8.56
waiting for the shop to open
to buy a cake tin

he carries scales
up the mountain

gets an ant on his finger
licks it off

you mention the family
who lost a child ...
a butterfly appears

twice as worse

she was called a blue stocking

*mention humanitarian aid
and the room empties*

*have you heard the good news that Iesu died for us
and rose again?*
no.

*I memorised everyone at St Vincent's
last name in my class*

wow!
the busker's only word

Fred
in sidewalk cement

people who use the word deplorable

snobs are those ill at ease with themselves?

golf balls & kangaroo dung

I like the word 'model'

it's a very looky sort of place

the whole car's a handbag

Seduced Hair

cowshit plaster for a pond?

Love, love me do!

the analyst said
I don't even know you

I get an electric shock from water

choke
on an imaginary conversation

I'm a zombie without a voice

they're all good people
I s'pose

bus stop, he shouts:
one church is enough!

I didn't want to get all feministy and human rightsy
about it

couplets
and shit

A dozen limmered ticks

The humming-birds hover in place
Like fairies, a magical race
      With the steadiest beak
      They feed all the week
Hanging from flowers like lace

An insomniac fellow named Bree
He had the most flexible knee
      He cradled his head
      With a leg round the bed
An advantage, I'm sure you'll agree

An optimist chappie called Spoon
Always wanted to fly to the moon
      He set out one day
      With a horse and a dray
And I'm told that he's coming back soon

A surrealist never can tell
If you're seriously ready to yell
      He tells you sky's white
      The land is a kite
And the sea is a freshwater shell

At two my sweet darling cried 'lunch!'
In a voice that was full of the crunch
      I knew she'd like eggs
      They're more peaceful than legs
And not nearly so tricky to munch

The members of poetry scenes
Would like to advise that they've been
      Neglected too long
      And will hold back their song
Until they are rich and pristine

In our assembly of poets
This righteous rabble of know-its
    It's not so much ego
    As long as you each know
That I wrote our loveliest sonnets

There are usually more poetry ladies
Than techno bands back in the eighties
    At workshops and festivals
    The perfumed confessionals
Of perhapses, it-could-bes, and maybes

The Canberra poetry men
Are mightily civil and then
    Add prizes and degrees
    Their obscure PhDs
And a liberal dressing of Zen

The ideals of the Anthropocene
Seem to border upon the obscene
    They give up on climate
    And just redesign it
In concrete without nature's sheen

There once was a tall academic
Researching a short epidemic
    He blamed it on protein
    But his data was so mean
It withered his lofty polemic

On an island we call the Galapagos
Lies a lizard with a massive oesophagus
    It balloons like a kite
    And swoops out of sight
And usually lands right on top of us!

work & play

dawn
a magpie sings
the eyes open

#love
this morning's
graffiti

cashpoint
the drunken man mumbles something about
policy

car wash
imagining
a massage

after a lively class
cleaning
the whiteboard

fun fair
a scream
at every turn

crickets ring
digging couch
at Lyneham Commons

a prison for magicians

they got it out of me ...

I stole her intuition
and used it as my own
(which you can't do)

it led me to the green
at lunchtime as the
prestidigitator spindled
and spiralled his clubs
into the caddy's arm
and pulled them out of the
hotelier's ear, with a receipt

I thought to learn some influential
morsel from the councillor
but it was too late
the game was won
and without common ground
drinks futile

however, I did my best
circulating with cards
and asking members to choose a secret
which I discerned
and whispered in their ear

I had them in my pocket then
with a handkerchief
a rabbit paw
and a dove

Voodoo Chile (slight return)

Jesus was a left-wing radical
socialised with prostitutes
tax-collectors and lost fishermen

women devoted themselves to him
as he devoted himself to them
his teachings snaffled by epistle-scratchers
made into religion and dogma—
when he talked about
forgiveness

if he was here now
he'd be Edward Snowden
or Malala

playing 12-string guitar
going for a big band sound
living in a bach in the Coromandel

he already came back once
as Jimi Hendrix
that's what he meant
when he got up at Woodstock and said
hmm, so we meet again

Afterword

The genesis of this book was my involvement with the Prose Poetry Project. At one stage I was writing prose poems about being a poet and what constitutes work for someone who must play in order to create. A number of these pieces were included in a critical/creative essay published in *Axon*, titled 'Vocation.Vocation.' Seeing this preoccupation, Shane Strange suggested putting together a book called *Work & Play*.

I wanted to contrast the prose poems with lineated poems, and for the second section delved into a file of work written in the couple of years before I came to Canberra (2012-2013), which contain similar themes. They begin with the poem 'Spring' and run to 'the candidate'. A number of these poems were consciously experimental, for example 'repechage' and 'Surdity' responded to a request I put out on facebook for suggestions for novel topics, my feeling being that some subject areas tended to be neglected by poets—this file was originally called 'Opening the box'.

The remaining poems are more recent and include three of what I call 'sem' poems, developed from a model I used in *semi* (the creative project for my PhD on semiotics and poetry). This strategy takes 'lines' of mostly spoken, found material and weaves together a loosely fitting sequence. Looking back, I can see that the poem 'Spring' is really the first poem which begins to appropriate in this way.

The title poem is a traditional haiku sequence, and 'displace' is based on haiku techniques but is more conceptual than haiku usually are—it was written for the critical/creative paper, 'Displaced metaphors: collaborative poetic responses to language in a postphysical world', with Ruby Todd and Lucinda McKnight, published in *TEXT*. The experience of teaching limericks to a group of new writers led to my composing a large number of them myself, a selection of which are included here. The two sections of lineated and prose poems are bridged by a haibun (prose and haiku), 'Broga, Bega'.

Notes

p. 22, 'Proem' is Subhash's term for the prose poem.

p. 23, Written after hearing Ania Walwicz read in Melbourne. Probably the most stunning performer of poetry I have ever heard, her work is notable for the fact that it is exclusively in the prose poem form.

p. 31, Jón Páll Sigmarsson was a power lifter who won the World's Strongest Man competition on four occasions.

p. 42, burras – burrows, or mounds of sand, one of the waste products of china clay mining. The burren – an area in the west of County Clare, Ireland.

p. 49, "The more I take care of myself the more prosperous I am"– Cheryl Richardson, at Healyourlife.com

Acknowledgements

Thanks to the editors and publishers of the following venues in which many of these poems previously appeared:

21st AAWP Conference Proceedings, Axon: Creative Explorations, Bukker Tillibul, The Canberra Times, The Cornish Banner/An Baner Kernewek, Deep South, Haibun Today, JAAM, Journal of Poetics Research, Landfall, Lyrical Passion, Mascara Literary Review, Otoliths, Poetry New Zealand, Rochford Street Review, Stride, TEXT: A Journal of Writing and Writing Courses, Uneven Floor; and in the anthologies *Seam: Prose Poetry Project* (IPSI, 2015), *Pulse: Prose Poems* (Recent Work Press, 2016) and *Tract: Prose Poems* (Recent Work Press, 2017).

Thanks to Shane Strange, Silvana Moro, members of the Prose Poetry Project, and Sue Peachey.

Owen Bullock is originally from Cornwall and lived for 25 years in Aotearoa, New Zealand before migrating to Australia in 2014. His publications include *semi* (Puncher & Wattmann, 2017), *River's Edge* (Recent Work Press, 2016), *A Cornish Story* (Palores, UK, 2010) and *sometimes the sky isn't big enough* (Steele Roberts, NZ, 2010). He has edited a number of journals and anthologies, including *Poetry New Zealand*. He recently completed a PhD in Creative Writing at the University of Canberra on the poetry of Alistair Paterson, Alan Loney and Michele Leggott.

2016 Editions

Pulse **Prose Poetry Project**
Incantations **Subhash Jaireth**
Transit **Niloofar Fanaiyan**
Gallery of Antique Art **Paul Hetherington**
Sentences from the Archive **Jen Webb**
River's Edge **Owen Bullock**

2017 Editions

A Song, the World to Come Miranda Lello
Cities: Ten Poets, Ten Cities Various
The Bulmer Murder Paul Munden
Dew and Broken Glass Penny Drysdale
Members Only Melinda Smith and Caren Florance
the future, un-imagine Angela Gardner and Caren Florance
Proof Maggie Shapley
Black Tulips Moya Pacey
Soap Charlotte Guest
Isolator Monica Carroll
Ikaros Paul Hetherington
Work & Play Owen Bullock

all titles available from
www.recentworkpress.com

www.ingramcontent.com/pod-product-compliance
Lightning Source LLC
Chambersburg PA
CBHW032048290426
44110CB00012B/997